T0083679

Landscape Portrait Figure Form

Landscape Portrait Figure Form
Dean Rader

OMNIDAWN PUBLISHING
RICHMOND, CALIFORNIA
2014

Cover art: Landscape Portrait Figure Form by Lora Fosberg, 2013

Cover and Interior Design by Peter Burghardt

Typefaces: Sabon LT Std and Futura Std

Offset printed in the United States
by Edwards Brothers Malloy, Ann Arbor, Michigan
on Glatfelter Natures Natural 55# Recycled 30% PCW
Acid Free Archival Quality FSC Certified Paper
with Rainbow FSC Certified Colored End Papers

Cataloguing-in-Publication Data is available from the Library of Congress

Published by Omnidawn Publishing, Richmond, California
www.omnidawn.com   (510) 237-5472   (800) 792-4957
10 9 8 7 6 5 4 3 2 1
ISBN: 978-1-890650-73-5

CONTENTS

THREE

Alle Kunst ist der Freude gewidmet

[All art is dedicated to joy]

—Paul Klee

ONE

AMERICAN SELF PORTRAIT

Give me the sheriff star pinned to the mermaid
and that tiny piece of wood from your throat.
Give me the saw blade, the plastic cat's eye.
Give me the flash drive of your tongue:

I want to save everything. Even the goat horns
you strapped to the skull of the little girl,
and yes, both of her hands. No, I don't really
know what that means, but so what?

I'll take the boneyard and all its yellow flowers,
I'll take the pisspot, the necklace of petal fire,
and while I'm at it, I'll take the body's wafer:
I'll take whatever breaks down beneath its own sad weight—

whether it's this life or a bad party. Your tangy
pelt, your twitch. You want my sandwich,
hey, get in line. This isn't the Army, but I'll march.
I want your shoulder holster, I want your mouth of bullets.

SELF PORTRAIT AS WIKIPEDIA ENTRY

Dean Rader was born in <u>Stockton, California</u> during the <u>Summer of Love</u>. His sorrow is his own. He believes in star-sting and <u>misnomer</u>; he carries a toy whistle in his pocket. <u>American</u> by nationality, he was conceived in a <u>Fiat</u> near the <u>Place du Châtelet</u>. If asked, Rader will lie and say he doesn't remember it, but his lazy eyes and hunched back give him away. His left <u>pinky finger</u>, broken from basketball, has never healed, which he attributes to the caesura of distance and longing. His heart, the size of a <u>normal</u> man's heart, has been used as a model for a forensic mannequin. As a young boy, he once carried a <u>small</u> package to the river, but it was the wrong address. If asked to describe the river, he quotes van Heisenstadt ("die grenzen des wasser nicht vom errinerung"). Rader is not the little cricket. He is not a scissors for lefty. His soul, the size of a tiny condom, slides quickly onto time's blind spot. In 2004, he was asked about time's <u>blind spot</u> but responded only that "time, like a bandage, is always already wound and unwound." Once, as a student in college, he grew a third sideburn. Darkness, his maquette, darkness, his morning coffee. Rader's father studied to be a mortician; his mother was a therapist and, not surprisingly, Rader pursued both. His head, matted with crude sketches of <u>benches</u>, <u>nipples</u>, and flower <u>petals</u> is roughly the size of the <u>Place du Châtelet</u>. Strong at math from an early age, he helped develop what has come to be known as the <u>Osaka</u> <u>Postulate</u>, which proves that the square root of asyndeton is equal to the inshpere of trespass, skin-spark, and elegy. As for his own spiritual beliefs, Rader is silent, though one of his recent poems, entitled "The Last Day of 34" suggests an <u>influence</u>

of Simone Weil ("community is work. // For all I know, God may be in both. / For all you know, God may be both) and Luigi Sacramone ("We want so much. // We only believe / in what we ask for"). Considered neither the lip blister nor the noodle wrench, Rader has emerged, at least somewhat, as the *repetitio rerum*. In more recent work, he <u>denies</u> this (though indirectly) citing instead his commitment to interlocutory boundaries (*bornage*) through what he calls the "phatic interstice." At present his voice, the <u>pitch</u> and <u>timbre</u> of a young girl's, asks only for Tang. Consumed by his charity work with the NGO Our <u>Uncle</u> of Instrumentality, he has stopped writing entirely. When questioned about this at a 2007 <u>fundraiser</u>, <u>Rader</u> quipped, "Let my words say what I cannot." Since then, a <u>fragment</u> of an unpublished poem attributed to Rader has started appearing on the <u>Internet</u>:

> Line up and line out
>
>   says the moonwhittle.
> Loss is the ring on our finger, the bright gem
> compassing every step as we drop down.
> Believe in what you know and you'll go blind.

Experts doubt its <u>authenticity</u>.

NOT LONG AFTER RICH: A STUDY

The will to be modern is more modern than
the will to be   Existence is a locomotive

pushing through a brush fire
in the mountains lost somewhere

between emergence and arrival.
Nothing is more indefinite than redefinition—

task and destruction—the still unbegun work
of repair   The undefiled snow on the slope

in winter is not a poem   She had

to get down from the blocked
train, her moment stricken eye, like her

tongue aflame. She will dive once more into
the difficult world. It will not be simple   It will

take all her thought. If you have burned once you
may still burn again. Raise it up there,

taste what has soared into the air.
You have a brutal thing to do

FRIGHTENED BY ASSASSINS, TOAD LISTS THE REASONS FROG SHOULD NOT WEAR JEWELRY IN HIS PORTRAIT

1. Metal detectors
2. It makes you easier to spot for assassins
3. The Sopranos
4. Your body wants to wear jewelry
5. You'd rather buy the flatscreen
6. Turtles hate necklaces
7. Remember the time you swallowed that ring?
8. It's all fake
9. Even the real stuff
10. The word bling
11. Man bracelets
12. It makes you easier to strangle (for assassins)
13. It's racist
14. Republicans
15. Can be used for GPS Tracking devices
16. Flies will see you coming
17. You'll always look single!
18. Number 12 is really worth two reasons
19. Show me an otter who wears pearls
20. Wallace Stevens, "Six Significant Landscapes" (stanza two)
21. Customs declarations
22. Look what happened to those Hobbits
23. Anniversaries
24. Because of all the robots
25. Questions

THE POEM CHOOSES ITS OWN ADVENTURE

And now the poem is on a bus somewhere in
Marrakesh scratching its way along one of
the old roads south of the Djemaa el-Fna. No
one recognizes it of course. The poem
is unshaven, sandaled, and wearing a poncho.
On its head a maroon fez. Who knows the last time
the poem bathed; it could be weeks. The poem smells
like your ass. If you want the poem to smell like
something else, you have to skip down seven lines.
You would not have chosen Morocco for the poem.
You hate sardine balls, and you're convinced people
only eat couscous because it sounds funny. The poem
is tired of you. It needed to get away. You ask so much
of it these days. Your demands are extravagant. You
wanted the poem to take you to Paris. You entertained
fantasies of coffee and croissants. You had even
spoken to your friends of *elan* and *joie de vivre*. When is the
last time you did anything for the poem? It's always about
you, still is you know. Even now in line nineteen, you can't
get past your own expectations. But the poem has needs of
its own. It's like a dog that was born on a leash. It's like
a dog. It's like a leash. Snap it on. Tell it to bark. Tell it to lie
down. Make it beg. You've forced it to sleep outside its whole
life, and now it's in a jungle in Bolivia, an ashram in Orissa, a
whorehouse in Amsterdam. You didn't even know you
wanted a poem with the word whorehouse in it, but the
poem did. And that's the difference. It's about care. It's

about attention. It's about giving, and let's face it: you are
a taker. And so the poem is golfing in Orlando, hiking in
the Alps. The poem is on the move. If you want a poem
about stasis, stop looking. If you want a poem that
surprises you, that inspires you, that rocks your world, you
have chosen the wrong poem. The poem has had it
with you. It's rolling a joint for Ginsburg, it's digging its
way out of the Dust Bowl, it's fighting for the Confederates,
it's helping Geronimo shoot a white man, it's killed Lewis
and is seducing Clark's wife. The poem picks evasion, it
selects erasure, it opts for abandonment. It wants you out
of its life. It's decided it was wrong about beauty. And though
it might be indifferent to love, it's coming back for glory. And
now the poem is in the back seat of a cab, your address in
its GPS. Its sideburns are longer, it's wearing a dress, its fur
glistens in the blue lights of the dashboard. It's on all fours.
You are fast asleep in front of the television. And now
it's line 45, and the poem is tired of playing games,
and so it has finally decided, despite everything
you might have expected, to end it all right here.

SELF PORTRAIT AS PHOTOGRAPH NEVER TAKEN

Here is the wind as it locks and reloads above
the waves. And there, the clatter of gulls scattershot

across the beach. Notice the couple caught in mid-laugh
as the little dog of time tags along behind them, its leash

a tink tink tink in the distance. What is life but dark
waters washing us up? Tide in and tide out. The sky

white as an angel's robe, the angel's robe strung up
somewhere between what we want and what blinds.

What are the chances I'll recall any of this
next week? How likely is it that the hour I

have my hook dug into will tear its tine from
your skin? Let's tell the carpenter to put down

his hammer. What do we care if the bell goes on
with its silent journey through hours? We can

build our own fire, string our own line. Maybe the sea
will peel back its waves, maybe the blackened boat

of the body will reel in the last rope from the pier,
maybe the fish, maybe the lone gull, maybe the moon

aswim in its minnow-bucket . . . Even if the stars
take it all back, even if the drummer drops his sticks

and walks into the ocean, even if the trees tie on
their bad blindfolds, we'll be okay. We don't need

anything except what we will remember, and even that
will change, like a cloud whose rain is about to fall.

Just wait. Someone is going to warn that boy against
building sandcastles so close to the water. It won't be me.

TWO

BECOMING KLEE, BECOMING COLOR

Instead of the endless exercise of
       the sketch, instead of the trace.

Instead of mimicking Manet from
       memory, instead of absinthe and

afterglow. Instead of the screaming skull.
       Instead of. Ask, he does, of tenor

and timbre, for the hand to unbutton
       color's blouse. Instead of blouse.

He finds he knows shapes the way the sea
       knows its waves: the thing it flows

in and out of. He sees crimson so clearly he
       becomes crimson, black with such

clarity he turns blind. Instead of image.
       Over and over he rides the color wheel

deep into his mind's night, hoping to arrive
       at the right shape. When he closes his

eyes he tries to want what the colors want:
       the agony of onyx, the sorrow of burlywood,

the obsessions of oxblood. Over and over he
    asks of the colors to find their form.

Instead of folding into augur. What the mind
    never stops seeing: sienna as square,

terre verte as rhombus, cyan circle as the viridian
    light of digon. The azure arbelos. As

though his own, he accepts triangle's sharp sin,
    he takes on the salvation of the little

oval. Instead of triquetra. Instead of annulus.
    Instead of plane or line, he requests

pattern but structures hide behind the colors
    that are not theirs. Harder than

lifting the waves from the seas themselves.
    He sees the seas so clearly but

is neither ocean nor its waves.
    Not even red becomes red.

Of the form it must figure, the body asks.
    Let coral cylinder be the angel's

rib cage, ochre lune the sun and its shadow
    self, a black and white incircle this

city and its roads, that instead of pushing
    us out, draw us in.

A PAGE OF SPRING
Paul Klee's *Ad Marginem* (1930)

I.
The sea's sky tides out
to lichen light and a stuck sun.
Night coils back and slurs.

Dawn tears into the weather, or
is it the weather that rips into fogshine:
the clouds' flicked
votives
and the leaves little wicks ignite.

II.
Once upon
a time

there was
no time

only
the page.

III.
Plants absorb light primarily using the pigment chlorophyll.
Cellular respiration allows for the conversion of light energy

15

To chemical energy. Palisade mesophyll. Stem and infiltration
Of stem. Terra and terawatt. Light begets the absence of light.

IV.
Once upon a page
there was no horizon,
only inversion.

In a world of margin, there is no margin.
Within the border there is no border.

We've moved on from the first idea,
never more acute than in its vanishing.

V.
Spindlestem, ropestem, ladlestem.
Heaven is always in the margin,
but in what direction?

VI.
The parts of a typical leaf include the upper

and lower epidermis, the mesophyll, the vascular

bundle(s) (veins), and the stomata(s).

VII.
Parchment of leaf-life, parched sugar sun,
Wind up and convert our lost letters,

Turn light into light, make our eyes
See the eye in sea and leaf light.

Crown of thistle thorn, we wear you
The way the sun wears the cross

We've nailed it to. The vascular
Bundle, God's other stoma,

Never bleeds out.

VIII.
You are upside down, not the bird.

VEDUTA AMERICANA
Paul Klee, *Landscape with Black Columns (1919)*

1) And they drift down from holes in the cliff, trot out
from behind the mesquite trees along the ridge,
and they crawl out of the little bunkers buried beneath
the sand, and they climb up from the ditches,
scale the banks of the arroyos, and walk through the
cactus, the limestone, and the ocotillo. They are sad
and hungry, and the desert is so cold.

2) and the desert is so cold, and they are so sad
and so hungry, and the sky has fired up its skillet,

and the ghosts have forgotten why they are here.

All they know is the black scaffolding of the world,
the divot of air after the lash on flesh.

3) And after the lash on flesh, the divot of the air, and after the
air the beginning of air, ghost of the air, ghost of the moon-
break and its pieces of glass, ghost of the thigh bone, ghost of
the farmer and ghost of the dog, ghost of the hammer, ghost of
the noose and the tree stump, ghost of the guitar, ghost of the
copper mine, ghost of the gold, ghost of the gods, ghost of the
devil, ghost of the pickaxe, ghost of the bean field, ghost of the
bride, of the groom, ghost of the groom, ghosts of the ghosts.

4) Of the ghosts, the ghosts say nothing.
   They all have the same voice.

5) the same voice in the same ear:
   we too like it slow.   don't turn around.
   they have it all wrong.   do you like my teeth?

6) my teeth and their ghosts
have made you their meal,

                         have made you.
Their meal is a bowl of whatever that
                  moment is when the rain ceased.

7) the ghost rain on the ghost crow on the ghost wire
   the ghost man, the ghost woman, her ghost mouth
   the ghost wind on its ghost feet
   the ghost chair, the ghost hand, the ghost beer
   the ghost snow tipped from its ghost bag
   the ghost angel
   the ghost book on the ghost desk, the ghost poem
   the ghost rhyme, the ghost stars in their ghost hats
   the ghost stars in their ghost glasses
   the ghost van on the ghost road
   the ghost horse and the ghost fence and the ghost lash
   the ghost cactus, its ghost thorns
   the ghost rain, the ghost rain, the ghost rain

TWENTY LINES ON PAUL KLEE'S *MAN IN LOVE*

In each stanza of this poem
There are five lines
One for the first time
I put my finger
On your bottom lip

One for the night
You slept next to me
For eight straight hours
Another for the next life
In which you'll kill me

One more for
Sorrows tiny knot
You may one day
Untie
And one last one

For that slice of sky
The heavy leaf the cupped
Hand the opened lip in
And into which we fall
Without belt or net

FORECAST

A storm is blowing in from Paradise; it has got caught in his wings with such a violence that the angel can no longer close them. The storm irresistibly propels him into the future to which his back is turned, while the pile of debris before him grows skyward. This storm is what we call progress.

Walter Benjamin on Paul Klee's *Angelus Novus*

I.
Origin is the goal.

II.
A weathervane
              all a-spin on the roof;
points everywhere at once.

Drunk with wind,
The angel keeps going in circles.

III.
The world's screen saver clicks off.
Everything reboots.

IV.
And you with rain on the inside
soaked beyond bone, beyond
                      the beginning of bone,
refuse to open the window.

V.
Don't worry, it's already here.

VI.
We know the past
only in relation to itself—

the future on the other hand,

VII.
The new angel will rise
and fall at the same time,
like a sequence of events inverted,

thunder and lightning,

                   the reverse,

then back again.

VIII.
Evolution is more than growth,
it's a mix of conservation
and revolution.

What does not happen,

                   cannot.

IX.
No match for the winds.

                    The angel's wings
beat at the storm the way the heart hammers
against cessation.

X.
        Stop.
Just for a second. The tornado
will carry you wherever
you want to go.

XI.
The prediction calls for
darkening skies, more wind,
heavy turbulence.

                Though we
are advised to remain grounded,
we take flight.

PAUL KLEE'S *WINTER JOURNEY* AT THE
BEGINNING OF SPRING

What's gone and what's past help should be past grief
—The Winter's Tale

No place the road leads is where it goes. Clouds and the
caravans of insects in motion across the quiet know this

and press on. Distance is the invention of those intent on
arrival; neither product nor process of land or impression.

What you leave behind may or may not be what you return for,
your journey an unbelievable course that led you through the

remote and the crushed, passed shoulder-slag and body-drop,
around the stretched and sprawled where you find yourself in

front of a painting, itself an imagined map of your own life,
once again in winter, as life always is, as is always the place you

hope to move out of. Reader, it is you I think about now that
you have arrived. We began so long ago, you and I, from such

different places, our seasons always the opposite of each other:
yours leaning against spring and mine tilting toward autumn,

yet we wear the same coat. Here, let me fix the top button. I'll
pull up the collar. Snow is beginning to fall, and we have a long

way to go. In the left pocket, you'll find a compass. It is not
this poem, which is about to end, unlike you, despite the fact

you now find yourself in front of a tombstone fixed in a grave-
yard you do not know. The sky has put itself on ice,

the lone tree a chalice-spike of ash. Reader, I want to apologize
for bringing you here. I know you thought we were headed

someplace else. I confess that I did as well. Grief is a
snow squall. It blinds but it too moves along. Do not be angry.

It might be cold, but I have left you the coat.

THREE

POEM IN WHICH THE READER SELECTS THE MOST APPROPRIATE OF THE FOLLOWING TITLES:

A) STUDY ON THE DISTANCE BUT INEVITABILITY OF WAR
B) CHIAROSCURO
C) SESSHU TOYO: AN HOMAGE
D) TABLUEU VIVANT
E) LANDSCAPE WITH CONVICTION AND INTERROGATION

Somewhere the stars
have clicked on their little lamps
and gone hunting.

Only in darkness can you see
the light.
            Only by drowning
do you learn to swim.

Nothing is harder to believe in
than belief, and yet here
we are,
            at it again,

never really knowing
if we are the arrow
or the bow.
            The moon

unwinds its scarf
and dives into the pond.
Nothing on the water

but the strange shadows
of this life.
                    I could
walk over to the edge

to look for whatever
I have lost,
but instead I'll lean

my grief against
two or three pines
                    and walk away.

STUDY OF THE OTHER SELF: AMERICAN
SELF PORTRAIT II

Distance and inward, light and
the reversal of light, retread
tread and footfall. So much and so long,
the little voice within the little voice
says.
        We all
hide somewhere, why not in ourselves?

Existence is nothing more
                        than experience divided by endurance.
The self is a bell in the mind's ear.

Think of me as the broken you—
the part of you you know needs
more than a splint and a bandage.
I am the fracture,
                the busted bone you refuse to lose.

I am that rhyme [there even when
I'm not], and you are the
intake after rhyme:
                        silence, echo, wave in
the wave of waves.

If sorrow was a cup of pudding,
if sorrow was the spike of light

on the little pond, if sorrow was the pond
and you were the spike of waves,

                              the little light in the silent

rhyme . . .

If life were a sling, it would
still break your arm. If your arm
was forgiveness, I'd break it again.

Believe me when I tell you
that there is nothing beyond
these words, that wall, your name—

Here, stick your arm through the bar,
I want to sign your cast.

RUSH

Hieronymus Bosch, *Der Haywain (The Haywagon)* Tryptich, 1485-90.

Dear Mr Bosch

I have been watching a homeless man stuff straw
        into the legs of his pants
We are in a park near a haystack he stands
        over the stack staring long
into the absence of what he had removed
        like a sculptor might gaze at
a block of granite after the excess cut
        away I think Mr Bosch
of the beggar on the front panels of *The*
        Haywain his stretched stick stopping
just above a scab of scattered bones as if
        he could wave it and make the
animal whole again but a black bird and
        a hungry dog want things to
stay as they are of course inside the painting
        the wagon has also stilled
as dozens of people grab at the hay with hands
        and hooks despite the fact that
a king and a pope sit atop the hay and
        the wagon is pulled by a
band of beasts and everyone perhaps even
        Jesus in the cloud above
wants what is taken away this morning a

report on poverty in
the United States said that there had never
been more people considered
poor even though nothing ever really goes
away Mr Bosch not in
this life desire is not a dog at the
door and hunger is no horse
asleep beneath the umbrella of heaven
it will not wake Mr Bosch
and walk backward into the reigns history
has held we all want to climb
up into something we cannot understand
even the man with the hay
dank in his pants even the lord lofted high
on his fortune of air an
alternative to and protection from the
avarice of the sod strewn
world which is to say Mr Bosch that this life
is no more than a basket
strapped to the back of a beggar but who am
I Mr Bosch to talk
about allegory want as you know is
neither icon nor idea
but invention a landscape molded and
made for the man the
unfortunate man who rushes through it

AMERICAN SELF PORTRAIT III
OR
WHAT THE POET THINKS OF INSTEAD OF WAR

Take off
          your dress of flame: the whole
world is raining.

  We can say
we are more than a trickle
of sun, but what, really,
do we want of surrender
                    but supplication?
     Our lives
are language, our desires
apophatic, but not in that
order.
     We want what
language won't do, and we
ask only what we
are prepared to live.
                    Period pause
and line loss, this is what
we're left with.
               You and
the imperiled present,
you and the glove box of
the body, you and memory's
ice cube:

What's in the glass?
the poem queries. Walk, the
garden commands. Stop here
the poem types. Language
like desire only pays attention
to syntax—everything else
is metaphor.
           Your skin,
for example,
           is the crocus sky I
fall in to, your dress the silk bell
in desire's ear, and,
              (are you still
with me?) your hands
                   the silver sun striking the match.

HOW WE SURVIVE: A TRYPTICH

I.
This morning I went for a jog
along the ocean wearing a cape
of starlight. The sky hummed
like a laptop just booted up, and
the ocean, well, the ocean had
opened early, so it was ready, it
knew what it wanted, which was
to be taken in and cradled like
a baby that had slept through
the night for the first time, and
so I ran toward the darkness I
knew I would split open, my cape
a sail of sky-shimmer against the
waves. Every dog on the beach
slowed to a trot, Frisbees and
tennis balls found their rightful
arc the only time that day. Even
the gulls circled back around a
second time, hoping to pedal
the tiny bicycle of light as it
rose and fell behind me. Hop
on, I say to my fears, who have
been trailing me since before
I began, let me carry you
everywhere you want to go.

II.

This afternoon I took a nap
wearing a costume that looks
just like me. Inside it I felt like
another person who happened
to know so many things about me,
like my preference for almonds over
cashews, how sometimes, when
I am in a strange room, I imagine
hopping from one piece of
furniture to the next, how often
I think about the time my
grandmother spanked me when
I was six, and what exactly my body
looks like to other people. Inside
me, it seems particularly bad that
I can tell you almost nothing
about the poverty line, or that I am
frequently unclear about the distinctions
among Hamas, Al-Quaeda,
Al-Fatah, and the Taliban, not to
mention the difference between
mass and weight, in part because I am
feeling very heavy right now, as though
I have begun sinking into myself the way
one falls into a deep sleep, both of my
selves dreaming that I will wake out of
the wrong body and walk uncovered
into the mistaken world, ill equipped
for anything except regret.

III.
Tonight I made love to you wearing
a suit of armor. I kept saying *armor,*
armor, *armor* over and over until you
reached up and closed the facemask.
Inside the helmet my voice hummed
like an engine on a long car ride,
my words driving me far into the
two-lane road of your body's night.
I tell you this even though I know
how much you hate it when
I recount the recent past, a
voice over telling us either what we
already know or what we want
to find out. But the world comes
to us in stories, and this is how I
narrate the scenes of this life and how
you mark my version of the night
against what really happened. This
is the way I make sense of darkness
and regret, how I let you know it's
okay to lift the mask and let me out.
It's how we survive, how we keep
going, or, at the very least, how we
know we haven't stopped, despite
the dogs at our heels and the little
hook of death deep in our skin.

APOCRYPHAL SELF PORTRAIT

"The Coldest Winter I Ever Saw Was The Summer I Spent In San Francisco"
attributed to Mark Twain but its origin(s) are unknown

The darkest night of my life was that morning in your car.
 My heart would not stop storming. You said it was

climate change. I may not be able to prove you wrong,
but that doesn't mean the end is near. The end is always

near. I read somewhere that the sum of the earth's water
will never change. Nothing is taken away, nothing added.

Every drop is the same age, every age dyed in the same
drop. The cut-up clouds stretched and strung out have

had about enough. Each day is a boat on a lake we row
ourselves into. We try to pick at the scab of sunlight

itching overhead, but we can't take our eye off the little
crack in the hull we know keeps growing. The Buddha

says everyplace we've been we stay. Right now, he's in
my dream sitting alone at an empty table, my tiny chair

about to collapse beneath him. Mark Twain walks into
the room looking exactly like Colonel Sanders. In one

hand, he cradles a bucket of chicken, in the other he
carries an ax. *The heaviest weight is the lightness of the soul,*

he says to the Buddha. *Give in to the dark*, the Buddha replies,
and you won't feel the darkness. The longest

drive we ever took was that evening we parked next
to the cliff. The sidereal dashboard, the cracked

windshield of the body. I want you to know that it
is never the darkest right before the dawn. I want

you to know the truth about everything.
I want you to know that this is not the end.

I want you to know that when those memories
drop down, my umbrella opens.

NOTES

American Self Portrait lifts a line from Charles Wright's "Envoi." Thanks to Simone Muench for engendering that larceny.

Not Long After Rich: A Study takes its form and title from Adrienne Rich's "Not Long After Stevens."

The Poem Chooses Its Own Adventure was an assignment for Poet's Choice and winks at Alexandra Teague's excellent "Choose-Your-Own-Adventure Poem."

Becoming Klee, Becoming Color is a response to the *Paul Klee at SFMoMA* exhibit at the San Francisco Museum of Modern Art, 2011. Klee (1879-1940) was one of the great artists of the twentieth century and a fine poet. Much of his writing on art theory focuses on "line," "form," "figure," and "syntax" making it sound very much like poetic theory.

Veduta Americana animates and reimagines Klee's *Landscape with Black Columns (Landschaft mit den schwarzen Säulen)*, 1919. "Veduta," Italian for "view," is a large-scale painting of a cityscape or landscape.

Forecast enters into conversation with Klee's *Angelus Novus* (1920) and Walter Benjamin's "Theses on the Philosophy of History" (1940).

Twenty Lines on Paul Klee's *Man in Love* is for Jill Ramsey.

Poem In Which the Reader Selects the Most Appropriate of the Following Titles enters into conversation with "High In The Mountains, I Fail To Find The Wise Man" by the great T'ang poet Li Po (701-762). Sesshu Toyo (1420-1506) is perhaps the most important master of ink and wash painting in Japanese history. He is best known for his *Long Landscape Scroll*. *Tableau Vivant* or "living picture" is a representation of a scene or painting in which the actors are silent and motionless.

And now to you, Reader: If you selected title A), the poem is for my father; if you selected title B), the poem is for Jane Downs and Marie Dern; if you selected title C) the poem is for Judy Halebsky; if you selected title D) the poem is for LeAnne Howe; if you selected title F) the poem is for the Clements Family of Newtown, Connecticut.

American Self Portrait III or What the Poet Thinks of Instead of War thanks Simone Muench for many things, including "Our lives are language, our desires apophatic," which is a slight modification of a line from Charles Wright's "Absence Inside and Absence."

How We Survive: A Triptych's middle panel enters into conversation with Matthew Zapruder's "Pocket."

Readers interested in the works of art mentioned in this book can view them at deanrader.com/landscape.

ACKNOWLEDGMENTS

I would like to thank the editors of the following journals, in which many of the poems—sometimes in different form and under different titles—first appeared: *American Literary Review*, *Boston Review*, *Fifth Wednesday*, *Kestrel*, *Lumn*, *The Minnesota Review*, *New American Writing*, *TriQuarterly*, and *Volt*. Special shout outs to the editorial staffs at *TriQuarterly*, *Wake*, and *Kestrel* for nominating some of the poems here for Pushcart Prizes. I'm particularly appreciative of Laura Cogan and Oscar Villlalon at *Zyzzyva* who first published "Self Portrait as Photograph Never Taken," "Twenty Lines On Paul Klee's *A Man In Love*," "Poem in Which the Reader Selects the Most Appropriate of the Following Titles," "Apocryphal Self Portrait," and Self-Portrait as Wikipedia Entry" (including an online version complete with hotlinks).

"American Self Portrait" was a finalist for the Poetry Society of America's Louis Hammer Award for 2011, judged by David Lehman. I'm grateful to David and the PSA for many things.

I would also like to thank Rusty Morrison, who is one of the best readers of poems around. I am also so grateful for Ken Keegan, Liza Flum, Gillian Hammell, RJ Ingram, and everyone at Omnidawn. Big kudos to the incomparable Peter Burghardt for his tireless efforts designing the book despite my tedious aesthetic demands. You are great ambassadors for poetry.

I am particularly indebted to Simone Muench for her smart and savvy contributions to many of these poems. Thanks also to Bruce Bond, Cristina Garcia, Timothy Donnelly, LeAnne Howe, Elizabeth Savage, Bob Hicok, Jonathan Silverman, Brian Clements, and Brandon Brown. Special thanks goes out to Poet's Choice and Chris Haven.

I can't say enough good things about Lora Fosberg or her art. It was a great privilege to collaborate with her on the cover, which is better and cooler than I could have imagined. Check out her stunning pieces at lorafosberg.com

Lastly, thanks to my family, here and elsewhere. This book is dedicated to Henry Michael Rader who was born about the time this baby entered its last trimester. I'm grateful for both.

Dean Rader's debut collection of poems, *Works & Days*, won the 2010 T. S. Eliot Poetry Prize, was a finalist for the Bob Bush Memorial First Book Prize, and won the 2010 Writer's League of Texas Book Award. Recent poems appear in *Best American Poetry 2012*, *Boston Review*, *TriQuarterly*, *Ninth Letter*, *Colorado Review*, and *Zyzzyva*, which is featuring a folio of his poems in their fall 2013 issue. Rader publishes widely in the fields of poetry, American Indian studies, and popular culture. He is chair of the English Department at the University of San Francisco.